DUCT
SHUI

D0816094

Duct Shui Masters
Jim and Tim—The Duct Tape Guys

DUCT SHUI

A new tape on an ancient philosophy

by *The Duct Tape Guys*

Workman Publishing • New York

Text: Tim Nyberg and Jim Berg
Design and illustrations: Tim Nyberg
Photography: Tim Nyberg

Cataloging-in-Publication information is available from the Library of Congress.

Workman books are available at special discounts when purchased in bulk for premiums and sales promotions as well as for fund-raising or educational use. Special editions or book excerpts can also be created to specification. For details, contact the Special Sales Director at the address below.

Workman Publishing Company, Inc.
708 Broadway
New York, NY 10003-9555
www.workman.com

Manufactured in China

First printing, March 2002

10 9 8 7 6 5 4 3 2 1

Acknowledgements

This is our fifth book! Obviously, we could not have written even one of our books without the existence of duct tape. So we would like to thank whomever it was back during World War II who first said, "You know what we need? We need a waterproof tape to keep the moisture out of these ammunition cases." Because at that moment duck tape was born. Once again, we would also like to thank our families and friends for their support and encouragement in our duct tape evangelism efforts. And to Duck® Products, a Henkel Group Company, for all the rolls of research material.

Feng Shui
(pronounced fUNG shWAY)
Composed of two words:
Feng (wind) and Shui (water)

Duct Shui
(pronounced DAHkt shWAY)
Composed of two words:
Duct (wind tube) and Shui (water)

What does all this mean?
Your guess is as good as ours!

DUCT
SHUI
INTRO

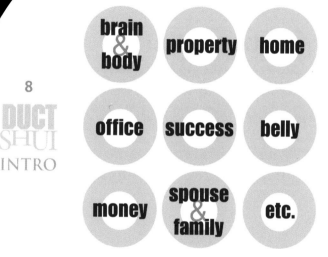

The Nine Zones of Duct Shui

Table of Contents

DUCT
SHUI
INTRO

Duct Shui: The Genesis

This whole Duct Shui thing started when our friend Ray Beckstrom lost his job as a pinsetter at Bob's Beef and Bowl to automation. I know what you're thinking: There have been automatic pinsetters since the 1950s or before. True, but Bob pays more attention to his hot beef sandwiches than he does to his four-lane bowling alley. At any rate, after forty years of pinsetting (he started when he was six), Ray didn't know which way to turn. Then one night around three in the morning, Ray saw an infomercial touting Feng Shui consulting as an up-and-coming career opportunity.

Before we knew it, Ray had grown a Fu Manchu moustache, had printed up some business cards, and was hanging around our houses taking notes, rearranging our rooms, digging up our yards, and telling each of us

how we needed to "cure" the "bad chi" that we had flowing around us.

We listened for three weeks as Ray ranted on and on about Feng Shui and how it could improve our lives. It was an incredible show. Ray was elaborating about this ancient Chinese philosophy as if he had signed up to sell Amway or something, not just some correspondence course.

Then, about three hours into our fourth week of listening to Ray, Jim lost it.

"This is the most bogus, superstitious bunch of drivel I've ever heard!" Jim yelled, throwing his arms up in the air. I was about to agree with him when he continued, "This is brilliant! It's our next book! We can create our own philosophy. We can call it Duct Shui!"

Ray was speechless, but my wheels were turning. Jim was right! If people were paying big bucks for ancient Chinese philosophy consultants, surely they would drop a few bucks on a brand-new philosophy that involved duct tape.

I turned to Ray and asked, "Ray, could you give us access to some of your Feng Shui course notes so we can formulate Duct Shui based on these old Feng Shui principles? We would be doing a real service to the Western world if we could take the essence of Feng Shui and fortify it with duct tape!"

Ray's $399 Feng Shui Manual

Ray scratched his head and crinkled up his lip, thus sticking some of his artificially blackened moustache hairs up his nose. "Sure, I guess," Ray said. "Do I get a cut?"

I assured Ray we would compensate him for his efforts. He slowly pushed his three-ring binder full of correspondence material (for which he had paid twenty easy installments of $19.95) across the table toward us.

Jim and I grabbed the Feng Shui binder and retreated to the garage. This book is the result of what we learned there.

First, Some Background Info

Throughout this book we refer both to sections of Ray's Feng Shui Consultant Correspondence Course Manual and to the bilge Ray dished out during his "sessions" with us. We follow these Feng Shui tidbits with our commentary and/or Duct Shui Corollaries, which are our improvements on some of Feng Shui's more questionable recommendations.

this symbol will identify our hints

From Ray's
FENG⊙SHUI
Correspondence Manual

DUCT
SHUI
INTRO

Feng Shui (*fung shway*) is an ancient Chinese art (or philosophy) that brings prosperity, happiness, and abundance. "Chi" is the energy the Chinese say pervades all life. Feng Shui properly positions you and your environment in relation to this "chi" energy, the result being that you achieve harmony and happiness.

We don't pretend to know the first thing about Chi or Feng Shui. But we do know duct tape. And we know that there is POWER in duct tape. You can hear the energy crackling when you rip duct tape off the roll. And we know that both of us have achieved massive amounts of happiness because of duct tape.

DUCT SHUI
INTRO

Jim (left) and Tim (far left)

Feng Shui uses a compass (like the one shown on the right) to show how the elements relate to all areas of life. This compass is called a **Pa Kua** (pronounced *Pa Kwa*). Home design discussed in this manual "will" refer to this compass, with the front door of the house being at the bottom or north position.

18

DUCT
SHUI
INTRO

There are obviously mistakes in this Pa Kua thing. For instance: The compass points are totally upside down and backwards (you'd think they made this stuff up in Australia). And the guys who designed it are missing air and wind in the elements (duh).

The Pa Kua

important reference page

Duct Shui also uses a compass-type approach to explaining stuff. We call our compass thing a Da Ktap (pronounced *DAHk-tAPE*). You will notice that the Da Ktap is much simpler, gets the compass correct, and has only one essential element that relates to all areas of life (duct tape). You will also notice that the eight sides, as in Feng Shui's Pa Kua, all center around success; however, the Da Ktap's eight areas of life are more closely related to real life. This book will focus on these eight areas.

The Da Ktap

another
important
reference page

DUCT SHUI
INTRO

In the center of the Pa Kua is the yin and yang symbol. This represents positive and negative, opposing yet complementary forces that compose all of nature. Yin (the white fish) symbolizes the passive nature; yang (the black fish) the active nature. Nothing is all yin or all yang. These energies must be balanced for perfect harmony to exist.

Page from Ray's Manual Showing Yin and Yang Symbol

In the middle of the Da Ktap chart is Duct Tape. This represents what Jim and I believe to be the perfect and ultimate energy, complete in and of itself. There are no fish involved.

According to Duct Shui, all must be given equal access to duct tape for perfect harmony to exist.

another (smaller) Da Ktap thing for your easy reference.

Chinese philosophers believe we are influenced by three realms in the universe: **Heaven**, **Earth**, and **Human**. The practice of Feng Shui attempts to manipulate these influences to make sure you get the most positive life experiences. Heavenly influences include climate, atmosphere, and timing/chance. Earthly influences include food, clothing, and shelter. Human influences are the people around you.

One Realm of Influence

In Duct Shui, there is basically one realm of influence: **the couch.** Some might call this teaching by its other name: laziness. We prefer to call it resourcefulness— utilizing duct tape to maximize our leisure time. Talk about balance and perfect harmony—a man and his couch!

(Note: Some women also find the couch alluring.)

The Couch

From Ray's
FENG☯SHUI
Correspondence Manual

Chinese philosophy pinpoints
five factors that are key to
success: **Fate** (destiny), **Luck**
(chance), **Feng Shui** (positioning
of yourself on the earth),
Charity (positive actions
derived from serving others),
and **Self-Improvement** (developing
character and moral standards).

FENG SHUI RAY SEZ:

"Fate, luck, charity, and self-improvement.
Sounds to me like they're recommending a visit
to the local bingo hall as a key to success!"

One Factor for Success

Duct Shui has only one factor that contributes to success: **Duct Tape**. Make sure you have plenty of good-quality duct tape. The simplicity of this philosophy allows you to get back to Duct Shui's realm of influence (the couch).

The three layers of good-quality duct tape:
1) Polyethylene coating
2) Tight-weave-fabric middle
3) Rubber-based adhesive

Duct Tape's Three-Ply Construction

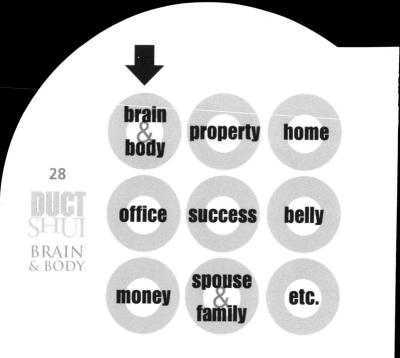

DUCT
SHUI

BRAIN
& BODY

brain
&
body

property

home

office

success

belly

money

spouse
&
family

etc.

DUCT SHUI

BRAIN & BODY

*Attaining focus, intelligence, energy,
and tranquillity through Duct Shui*

Like duct tape, your brain and body
are powerful tools. If you can harness
their powers, there's no telling what you
can achieve. Here are some easy ways to
train your brain and body using duct tape.

From Ray's
FENG☯SHUI
Correspondence Manual

Perform better in your daily
life by reciting this mantra:
**Gate gate, Para gate, Para
sum gate, Bodhi swaha.**
(Pronunciation: *GAH-tay GAH-tay,
PAIR-uh GAH-tay, PAIR-uh SUM
GAH-tay, BOH-dee SWA-ha.*)

DUCT
SHUI
BRAIN
& BODY

FENG SHUI RAY SEZ:

"When I first heard about this mantra thing
being recited by practitioners of Yoga, I couldn't
figure out what that little guy in *Star Wars* had
to do with it. Then I remembered that little
guy's name was Yoda, not Yoga."

Duct Tape Mantra

We have found no two words better for meditation than **DUCT** and **TAPE**. Follow the simple exercise described on the next two pages and you will achieve a state of perfect peace.

DUCT
SHUI
BRAIN
& BODY

DUCT SHUI

BRAIN & BODY

Reciting the Duct Shui Mantra

Try This Simple Exercise

Sit with your legs crossed (unless, like us, you have lost your youthful flexibility; then just lie on the couch). Close your eyes. Whisper the words DUCT TAPE, DUCT TAPE, DUCT TAPE (pronunciation: DAHk-tAPE, DAHk-tAPE, DAHk-tAPE) slowly about fifty times. You will notice that you have achieved a state of total tranquillity (or, if you are like us, that you have fallen asleep). *See illustration on page 32.*

DUCT
SHUI
BRAIN
& BODY

You can improve your children's academic performance by locating their rooms and bed position according to their birth charts.

DUCT SHUI

BRAIN & BODY

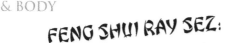

FENG SHUI RAY SEZ:

"I lost the birth chart portion of my Feng Shui manual. I think I'm a scorpion or something. All I know is I sleep curled up. Maybe it was a snail . . ."

Sleep Is Critical

Duct Shui also realizes the value of a correct sleeping position. We know from experience how uncomfortable that stiff neck can be if you fall asleep in the wrong position. To make sure you stay in a correct sleeping position, duct tape yourself to the bed.

Duct tape your kids to the bed so they don't toss and turn so much. Plus, they won't be able to come and wake you up for yet another glass of water.

Sound Spousal Slumber

DUCT SHUI

BRAIN & BODY

Your sleep position can increase your tendency to snore and that can negatively affect your spousal harmony.* We find that we snore more if we are sleeping on our backs. We suggest duct taping a volleyball onto your back so you have to sleep on your side or stomach. Presto! You've cured that annoying snoring!

*We will be dealing with more spousal harmony issues in the Spouse & Family section (see pages 187 through 203).

Secure Slumber

To boost your feeling of security while you slumber, sleep with a roll of duct tape on your bedside table. If you still don't feel secure, go around the house and duct tape all of the doors and windows shut. If light is bothering you, duct tape your eyes shut.

Ultimate Room-Darkening Shades

From Ray's
FENG ☯ SHUI
Correspondence Manual

To boost your vitality, place a bright red cloth between the mattress and box spring of your bed.

DUCT SHUI
BRAIN & BODY

FENG SHUI RAY SEZ:

"Be careful with this one! I heard about one guy that used a red and white checked cloth and he alternated between feeling wide awake and totally wiped out in ten-minute increments all day long."

Wake Up Alert and Refreshed

To wake up with a burst of energy, place a strip of duct tape on your back and connect it to your bed. When you get out of bed, the tape will rip off your back hair and get your blood coursing through your veins in no time! Or tape your eyes wide open so you look alert.

Achieve a Wide-Eyed Look

Brain Magnet Headband

Attract Positive Energy

Feng Shui deals with attracting positive energy. Duct Shui likes positive energy, too. Attracting positive energy to your brain is easy with a brain magnet—sticky-side-out duct tape around your head. *See illustration (A).* With this technique, you can suck in knowledge and wisdom from all those around you through a process similar to **osmosis.** *

WARNING: It is important to note that some negative energy and thoughts might also stick to this brain magnet. To protect yourself, it may work to put a square of duct tape sticky-side-in on your forehead. *See illustration (B).*

* No relation to Donny and Marie.

DUCT
SHUI
BRAIN
& BODY

Energize Your Thoughts

Just thinking about duct tape should get your mind whirling. If you find yourself in a funk, like you have a gray cloud hovering around your brain, try a **duct tape roll rip.** Aggressively rip about sixteen inches of tape off the roll. The sound of duct tape energy being emitted from the roll will energize your thoughts.

AMAZING FACT

The brain is the source of wisdom. In Feng Shui, the elephant symbolizes wisdom. Elephants are gray. Most duct tape is gray. Coincidence? We don't think so!

Expand Your Mind

Nothing says creativity and mind-expanding power better than a roll of duct tape. Examine the roll. See? No instructions. Let your creativity run wild!

DUCT
SHUI
BRAIN
& BODY

Guy with Expanding Mind

Putting books where you can see them as you enter the front door of your home will stimulate learning in both you and your children.

DUCT SHUI

BRAIN & BODY

FENG SHUI RAY SEZ:

"If you don't got no books, you can pick 'em up real cheap at the thrift store. Then you just pile 'em up in your entryway. Walla! You got yourself some smart kids."

Recommended Reading

Putting our Duct Tape books (and we'd recommend our videos, too) out where you can see them, anywhere in your house, will indicate that you have an appreciation for the finer things in life and are attempting to pass along your good taste to your children.

Positively Influence a Child

To cultivate a love for duct tape in your child:

1) Hang a roll or two over the crib instead of those plastic mobiles. This will cause the child to become fixated upon the intrinsic beauty of duct tape.

2) Give the child a roll to play with in its crib instead of conventional baby toys. This will give baby a feeling of superiority and self-confidence, develop dexterity, and enhance creativity.*

*Assuming that duct tape is not a part of a complete diet, and could present a choking hazard, we suggest parental supervision during the cultivation process.

DUCT SHUI BRAIN & BODY

3) Use duct tape as a reward for your child's positive behavior.

Generic Child

If you follow these three simple steps, you will find that your child's brain will eventually develop an addiction to duct tape (this is a good thing). Who knows, if you are lucky, your child might even grow up to be a Master Duct Shui practitioner.

DUCT
SHUI
BRAIN
& BODY

DUCT SHUI

BRAIN & BODY

Your house is like your body. A skylight in the ceiling is like having a hole in your head. This could mean that you will have an accident involving your head. Adding a skylight to an existing house is asking for trouble. You can cure the presence of a skylight by hanging a multi-faceted crystal sphere from the center of the skylight.

FENG SHUI RAY SEZ:

"One time I fell through Vern's skylight when I was scrapin' off the snow, and I cut my head."

Treating a Hole in Your Head

The best way to treat a hole in your head is to duct tape over it until you can get to the emergency room.

Treating Your Skylight

A leaking skylight can usually be fixed with (what else?) duct tape—it's like caulk on a roll.

Prevent acorn and hail damage before it happens by taping over the entire skylight immediately after installation.

DUCT SHUI

BRAIN & BODY

Place all five elements—fire, earth, metal, water, and wood—in a room to create power and enhance creativity. Make sure you place them in the proper order. If out of order, the improper relationship of the elements will result in bad energy.

The Five Elements (in correct order)

Only One Element Required

Keep it simple! Place just one element—duct tape—everywhere you look. This definitely inspires us and we guarantee* it will inspire you, too. (Since in Duct Shui there is only one element, placement order doesn't matter.)

DUCT
SHUI
BRAIN
& BODY

*Guarantee award reimbursement limited to a reimbursement of $75.00 (U.S.). Please note that written guarantee is not included in the purchase price of this book.
To obtain your certificate of written guarantee of inspiration obtained from the use and presence of duct tape, please send a certified check in the amount of $89.95 (U.S. funds) to:
The Duct Tape Guys, Guarantee Department
P.O. Box 130066, Roseville, MN 55113

Expel Negative Energy

DUCT SHUI

BRAIN & BODY

If you want to avoid the accumulation of negative energy and at the same time get rid of negative energy that has built up in your body, we suggest that you cover yourself entirely in nine layers of duct tape and attach a copper grounding cable to the nearest water main to siphon off the flow of electrical charges from your body.

WARNING: Do NOT try this during an electrical storm.

The "Barn Door" Dilemma

We were just thinking . . . If Feng Shui likens a house to a body, it would stand to reason that leaving the front door open is akin to leaving your fly undone. This can be "cured" with the simple application of one strip of duct tape (a remedy that works even if your zipper is broken).

DUCT
SHUI
BRAIN
& BODY

Pants with Duct Shui Zipper Cure

DUCT SHUI
PROPERTY

Duct Shui fixes for problem yards and poorly placed houses

Physical surroundings are very important in the practice of Feng Shui. In Duct Shui they don't matter. In fact, we don't understand what Feng Shui Masters are getting so worked up about. Here are our simple suggestions to help them lighten up.

DUCT
SHUI
PROPERTY

From Ray's
FENG☯SHUI
Correspondence Manual

The ideal position for a house is in the center third of a rectangular lot with a protective hill behind.

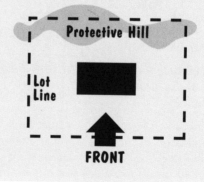

Ideal House Position

Move Those Lot Lines

If your house is not in the center third of a rectangular lot and you want it to be, the blatantly obvious thing to do would be to redraw the property lines with duct tape. Making the duct-taped property lines sticky-side-up also has the added benefit of keeping out common yard and garden pests.

PROPERTY

Make a Protective Hill

If you think having a protective hill behind your house is important and you don't have one, you can easily make one with duct tape. Just create large sheets of duct tape (camouflage duct tape works great for this) and drape them over trees (this cuts down on your fall raking time).

Lacking trees? Drape your duct tape tarp over a tall fence.

Landfill Protective Hill

Here's a better idea: Save big money by halting your garbage service and dumping your trash behind your house. When the garbage has reached hill height, duct tape over it. Many municipalities have utilized these "landfills" with great success. Some have even made ski hills out of their old garbage dumps. And remember, duct tape and Bubble Wrap® can turn any item of apparel into fashionable skiwear.

DUCT SHUI
PROPERTY

From Ray's
FENG☯SHUI
Correspondence Manual

Living on a sloping or a one-way street tends to create quick-moving energy that sucks good energy away from your home. Slow the flow of chi by planting bushes along the front of your property or placing an odd number of pinwheels or wind socks along the front of the property.

DUCT SHUI
PROPERTY

AMAZING
FACT

Speaking of wind socks . . . In just ten minutes, a hurricane releases more energy than all the world's nuclear weapons combined.

Slowing Energy

To slow down stuff whizzing past your house, wrap each post of your fence with sticky-side-out duct tape. If you don't have a fence, apply duct tape sticky-side-up to your sidewalk.

Traction Required

If your house is on a sloping street or a steep driveway, wrap your vehicle tires with duct tape, sticky-side-out to provide better traction.

DUCT SHUI
PROPERTY

Dangerous Energy

DUCT SHUI PROPERTY

On second thought, forget our hint on page 61. If you have energy flowing out of your yard, we doubt that a little shrub will stop it (even if it is wrapped in duct tape). Drop everything and call 911 or your local power company. Let professionals deal with loose electrical energy!

*Don't Touch Anything
That Looks Like This*

Slowing Energy Part Deux*

Speaking of slowing energy, you can slow the flow of energy and decrease your electric bill at the same time by duct taping over your light switches. This will cause you to think twice before flicking on the lights.

PROPERTY

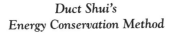

*Pardon our French. Tim can't pass up an opportunity to use his deux (two) years of high-school French.

*Duct Shui's
Energy Conservation Method*

From Ray's
FENG⊙SHUI
Correspondence Manual

64

DUCT
SHUI
PROPERTY

A stuffed storage shed becomes
a negative force on your property.
Keep it tidy and clean.

A storage shed in the Wealth Area
of your property symbolizes
increased
accumulation
of wealth.

Wealth Area with Storage Shed

Stuff That Shed!

To a duct tape pro, a stuffed storage shed is normal (in fact, desired). Duct tape can be used to hang stuff from the shed ceiling to create even more storage space. Furthermore, a storage shed stuffed with duct tape, located anywhere on your property, should be considered a positive force. This symbolizes that you are ready to deal with any situation that comes your way.

PROPERTY

From Ray's FENG⊙SHUI Correspondence Manual

If you live on a dead-end street, there is a lack of energy flow. To stimulate the flow of chi, create new activity by putting wind chimes and bird feeders in your yard.

DUCT SHUI PROPERTY

FENG SHUI RAY SEZ:

"You can make your dead-end street into a through street in no time by calling Jerry's Dirt Moving Service. Cripes! He charges only sixty bucks a day!"

Dead-End Thinking

Excuse us, but isn't the whole point of living on a dead-end street to achieve a lack of energy flow? If you want energy flow, live on the side of a freeway. Use duct tape to reinforce your windows so they don't rattle when semi trucks pass your house.

As for attracting birds into your yard, we've got that covered. Turn the page.

Duct Shui and Birds

DUCT SHUI PROPERTY

To attract birds to your yard, duct tape plastic decoy birds to your birdbath. To create more attractive housing for birds, re-side and reroof their houses with duct tape. To prevent real birds from soiling roofs and windows with their droppings, duct tape little diapers onto them.
See illustration (A).

Decoy Birds Attract Real Birds

From Ray's
FENG⊙SHUI
Correspondence Manual

If you share a driveway, put
a light at the point where the
driveways split to prevent the
loss of positive chi. Light
both sides of your driveway to
heighten the effect.

DUCT
SHUI
PROPERTY

FENG SHUI RAY SEZ:

"How's this for an idea: Duct tape some of them battery-operated camping lights on both sides of your car so you are safe from the energy loss wherever you travel!"

An Ounce of Prevention

Lights or no lights, if you have neighbors living this close, there is bound to be trouble! If you share a driveway, cover both sides of your car with duct tape to prevent scrapes and door dings (this is especially important if you and your neighbor share the same work schedule).

Duct Shui Auto Body Side Protection

DUCT
SHUI
PROPERTY

Stacks of Duct Tape Welcome Visitors
(tape not shown actual size)

Create Energy Columns

Nothing says positive energy like two majestic columns of duct tape rolls on either side of your driveway. It also makes it easier for the Publisher's Clearing House people to spot your driveway when they come with that big check!

DUCT SHUI

PROPERTY

If your front door is hidden from the street, put a large convex mirror where it will reflect the front door to approaching visitors.

Lighting the pathway also helps create maximum energy flow to your front door (and into your life).

DUCT
SHUI
PROPERTY

A Duct Shui Pathway

Lining the pathway to your front door with red duct tape says, "We have rolled out the red carpet for you." Better yet, cover your entire walkway with silver duct tape and the bright glow of the silver lining will cheer all who enter.

Note: This hint also helps prevent ants and weeds from establishing their homes in the cracks of your sidewalk. It may also prevent damage to your mother's back caused by inadvertently stepping on cracks.

DUCT SHUI PROPERTY

Show Your Visitors the Way

You can also put large duct tape arrows on the driveway pointing the way to the front door. Then again, if a visitor is not capable of finding your front door, do you really want them visiting you anyway?

DUCT
SHUI
PROPERTY

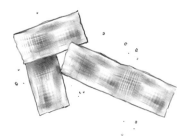

It's easy to make attractive arrows with just a few strips of duct tape.

Duct Tape Arrow

Or, Mislead Them

If most of your visitors are door-to-door salesmen, annoying neighbor kids, or teams of white-shirt-and-tie-clad peddlers of a religion in which you have no interest, make the duct tape arrows lead down your sidewalk, across your front lawn, past your driveway, and into your neighbor's yard.

DUCT
SHUI
PROPERTY

78

DUCT
SHUI
PROPERTY

If there is a tree blocking your front door, you don't need to cut it down. Use this cure: On a circular piece of red writing paper, with a new ink pen, write the words *"Raise head, see happiness."* Post the paper on the tree at eye level or higher.

Enter Through the Tree

If you have a tree blocking your front door, allow the tree to grow large enough to cut a tunnel through it (like those giant redwoods in California). Then, line the inside of the tree tunnel with duct tape so you don't get full of slivers and tree sap every time you walk through it.

DUCT SHUI
PROPERTY

DUH!

**DUCT
SHUI
PROPERTY**

If there is a tree blocking your front door, and you don't want to wait until it grows to tunneling size, there is still no need to cut the tree down. Use this cure: Duct tape a sign to the tree that says, "Use back door."

A Sign Cures Stupid Tree Placement

From Ray's
FENG☯SHUI
Correspondence Manual

82

DUCT SHUI
PROPERTY

Cul-de-sacs are bad because chi flows in and circulates, sucking the positive chi out of the surrounding homes. To remedy this, put a windmill or fountain in the center of the cul-de-sac.

Fountain

Cul-de-Sac with Fountain

Favorable Circles

It's no coincidence that cul-de-sacs are favorable in Duct Shui. After all, the words CUL-DE-SAC and DUCT TAPE contain many of the same letters, and a cul-de-sac actually resembles a roll of duct tape. Besides that, it's fun to duct tape your steering wheel hard to the left and see how long you can go around in circles on the cul-de-sac without going up onto the neighboring lawns.

DUCT
SHUI
PROPERTY

DUCT SHUI
PROPERTY

Create This Stunning Fountain

Cul-de-Sac Fountain

Sure, a fountain in the middle of your cul-de-sac is a charming addition to the neighborhood, but it can be expensive. Making your own fountain can be a fun Saturday project. Just duct tape together three old tires, a small pump, a tree branch, and a garden hose.

DUCT
SHUI
PROPERTY

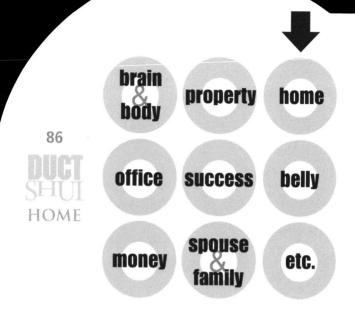

DUCT
SHUI
HOME

DUCT SHUI
HOME

*Decorating and energizing your
home with duct tape*

Feng Shui practitioners make huge bucks
by coming into your home and telling you
how to rearrange it for the acquisition of
positive chi (energy). Not us! We give you
a mess of valuable Duct Shui hints—all for
the minuscule price of this book.

DUCT
SHUI
HOME

A fundamental factor of Feng Shui
is cleanliness in your home.
A multifaceted crystal sphere
hanging in the Knowledge Area
of your home (front left corner
as you are facing the front
door) or over the head of your
bed will help you become neater.

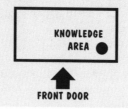

The Knowledge Area of Your House

On the Other Hand . . .

Since a fundamental factor of Feng Shui is cleanliness in the home, it's no wonder that we don't understand beans about it. The fundamental factor in Duct Shui is apathy (the total lack of desire to fix something the right way). If you possess this quality, you are well on your way to becoming a Duct Shui Master. *See page 223 for steps to becoming a Duct Shui Master.*

DUCT
SHUI
HOME

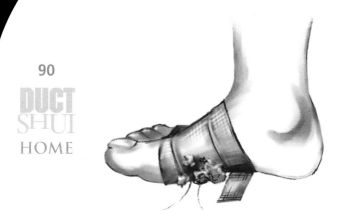

Declutter Your House the Easy Way

On the Other Foot . . .

To help you become neater, duct tape your feet and your guests' feet, sticky-side-out. As you walk around the house, you will be doing the vacuuming and picking up all sorts of loose items. You can easily sort what you have picked up and throw the junk away.

DUCT
SHUI
HOME

From Ray's
FENG☯SHUI
Correspondence Manual

A metal wind chime in the front area of your home (or office) will summon people to help you.

**DUCT
SHUI
HOME**

FENG SHUI RAY SEZ:

"One of the nice features of my Feng Shui course is that they get you started in their multi-level wind chime business. I get 30¢ for every wind chime I sell and 5¢ from every sale made by those under me in my organization."

Save your money! You can make this attractive wind chime by duct taping forks and spoons to a stick and taping the stick to your house's fascia.

A Simple Yet Elegant Homemade Wind Chime

How to Summon Help

To us, the sound of wind chimes says, "I'm at peace." If you really need to summon help, what you want to do is get some duct tape stuck in your hair, then rip it out. Your screams will most certainly draw attention.

A Guy About to Summon Help

To Help the Elderly

To summon help for the elderly, you could buy one of those medical alert things like on the television commercials where the lady has fallen and can't get up. Or, you could avoid the need to summon help by duct taping your elderly upright in their chairs.

(Not endorsed by the AARP—yet.)

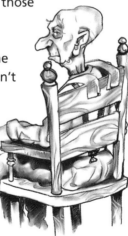

Prevent the Elderly from Falling

From Ray's
FENG☯SHUI
Correspondence Manual

Smooth out your life path and relieve anxiety and frustration by making sure your front door doesn't squeak or scrape the floor.

DUCT
SHUI
HOME

FENG SHUI RAY SEZ:

"This would explain why my life has been so frustrating. My front door squeaks something awful. But it does alert me to intruders. So I just keep it that way."

First Remove Anxiety

As far as we can figure, anxiety has little to do with the front door of the house (unless you've committed a crime and expect to be arrested at any moment). To relieve anxiety, we suggest that you place one roll of duct tape in every room of the house and use it often.

DUCT
SHUI
HOME

Then Remove the Door Squeaks

WD-40® will stop your front door from squeaking. As for the scraping on the floor, that's just something that naturally occurs when you have your brother-in-law help you build your house. Cover up the scrapes on your floor with duct tape. We suggest using camouflage duct tape if you don't want people to notice.

From Ray's
FENG☯SHUI
Correspondence Manual

If your guest bedroom is in the front of the house, your guests won't overstay their welcome. If it is in the back of the house, they may be there for a while.

DUCT
SHUI
HOME

FENG SHUI RAY SEZ:

"That does it! I'm moving my mother-in-law's bedroom to the front porch."

DuCT SHUI COROLLARY

Add a Guest Room

If you aren't concerned with this problem because you don't have a guest room, consider building a guest suite. Sound expensive? Not with refrigerator boxes and duct tape!

Remove Unwanted Guests

Duct tape your guests' suitcases shut. This should give them a clue that they are not welcome to stay overnight.

Or duct tape small stones to the mattress of your guest bed. Your guests won't overstay their welcome—they may not even make it through the first night.

DUCT
SHUI
HOME

If there is a corner of your house that is missing because of an indent in the outer wall design (see below), fix it with a smooth rock or statue at the corner to complete the area.

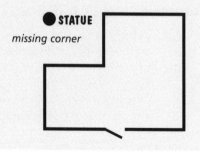

House with Missing Corner

Quick Fix for Storm Damage

If there is a corner of your house that is missing because of a windstorm, a tornado, or a bad driver, you can make temporary walls with refrigerator boxes and duct tape. Heck, if you use enough duct tape, they just might become permanent walls.

missing corner

Another House with a Missing Corner

If you have a missing or broken stairway banister, it will create feelings of lack of control in your life. The simple cure is to fix it or replace it with a good solid handrail.

DUCT
SHUI
HOME

FENG SHUI RAY SEZ:

"I'm starting to feel pretty stupid for paying $399 for this stuff. Heck, I can watch Norm Abram for free on TV."

DUCT SHUI COROLLARY

Hold on, Bubba!

If you have a broken post in your stairway banister, the sure cure is duct tape liberally applied to the missing post area. If your banister is totally missing, leaving you with nothing to hold onto, wrap your feet with duct tape, sticky-side-out, to give your feet a better grip.

DUCT SHUI HOME

From Ray's
FENG SHUI
Correspondence Manual

**DUCT
SHUI
HOME**

Bring more positive chi into your home by keeping the entry area of your home free of clutter *(see below)*.

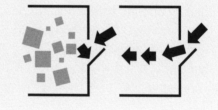

*Clutter-Blocked Energy (left) and
Free-Flowing Energy (right)*

Rippin' Good Energy

We've already dealt with the clutter issue *(see page 91)*. As far as bringing positive energy into your home . . . the sound of duct tape being ripped off the roll exudes more positive energy than anything we know of. So, hire a neighbor kid to stand in your entryway and rip duct tape off the roll into a PA system aimed at your front door.

FENG SHUI RAY SEZ:

"Now that I've read the Feng Shui information on the left, I've gotta correct something I said earlier. Do NOT pile up books in your entryway as I suggested on page 44."

106

Neighboring rooflines facing the front of your house are "poison arrows" that threaten

Ba-Gua mirror

your future. Reflect these poison arrows by placing wind chimes (hung with red cord in a multiple of nine inches) near your front entrance. Or, you may hang an octagonal "Ba-Gua" mirror above the front door of your home.

Page from Ray's Manual Showing a Ba-Gua Mirror

Avoid Implements of Harm

If you are afflicted by "poison arrows," "bullets," "catapulted stones," and other "implements of harm" . . . move!

Duct tape makes an excellent sealing device for moving boxes. It's strong, you can rip it with your bare hands, and you can label with it, too!

As you leave your house, yell "BAAA! GWAAA!" at the people shooting the stuff at you.

The positioning of your toilet back-to-back on a common wall with a bed is bad because the flushing sucks positive energy. To remedy this, put a mirror behind the headboard of the bed with the reflective side facing the wall.

**DUCT
SHUI
HOME**

AMAZING
FACT

The first toilet ever seen on television was on *Leave It to Beaver.*

Handy Commode

If your bed is on a common wall with your toilet, it means that you don't have that far to walk to go to the bathroom in the middle of the night. In fact, we suggest that if the common wall doesn't have a door in it, you cut a hole for even easier access. Then frame the hole with duct tape and avoid the need for that costly finishing carpentry.

No More Sucking Action

**DUCT
SHUI
HOME**

If you don't want the toilet sucking (which pretty much defeats its purpose), we suggest flushing a huge duct tape ball or two. This will certainly stop the effectiveness of the toilet's drain.

One Last Thought About Toilets and Mirrors

If you really think that a toilet can suck positive energy, and that a backwards mirror stuck behind your bed's headboard can reflect negative energy, duct tape the word "fool" onto your bathroom mirror.

112

If your bedroom is located over a garage, the cold, empty garage space is separating your bedroom from the "vital grounding energy" of the earth. A remedy for this is to paint a tree on the garage wall with roots painted on the floor, a large, healthy trunk up the wall, and branches and leaves on the ceiling under your bedroom.

DuCT SHUI COROLLARY

Ground Yourself

We had no idea that it was vital to ground yourself while you sleep!

If you really want to be close to the "grounding energy" of the earth, we suggest that you sleep in a ditch or duct tape yourself to a tree at night.

Suddenly More Room!

The Feng Shui fix to this "problem" requires far too much artistic talent for the average person. Do what Jim did when he read about it: Move your bedroom to the garage and park your car outside. This "cure" frees up your former bedroom as another place to store your rolls of duct tape. To protect your car from the elements, cover the entire vehicle in duct tape.

The average household has 1.5 rolls of duct tape. Jim's house has 42.3 rolls of duct tape on any given day. Tim comes in a close second with 29.0756 rolls.

A New Art Medium Is Born

If you do happen to have an artistic bone in your body, and wish to follow the Feng Shui advice, don't paint the tree in the garage; instead, use brown and green duct tape. Duct tape art is a wonderful artistic medium that requires no brushes, nor the cleanup associated with paint.

Tim's Duct Tape Art, "Triptych"
(see more duct tape art at ducttapeguys.com)

From Ray's
FENG☯SHUI
Correspondence Manual

116

DUCT
SHUI
HOME

If your bedroom has an exterior door, it can lead to relationship problems, financial depletion, or ill health. It also introduces an excess of chi into the room.

Cure this problem by putting a wind chime at the exterior door. It will regulate the flow of energy.

Too Much Chi?

We don't fully understand chi, but if too much of it is a problem, we doubt that a flimsy little wind chime is going to stop much of anything. We suggest that you duct tape over the exterior door of the bedroom. Or, for a less permanent fix, duct tape a bedsheet in front of the door. This will allow the door to be used in case of an emergency.

Chime Clanger Calmer

By the way, if you are placing wind chimes everywhere that Feng Shui experts suggest, you are probably close to getting arrested for disturbing the peace. And you certainly aren't getting any sleep because of all the clanging noise. To muffle the noise, wrap duct tape around the chime pipes or tape the clanger to the wall *(see diagram on right)*.

DUCT SHUI HOME

DUCT SHUI HOME

Diagram on Right

DUCT
SHUI
HOME

To determine if chi can flow
freely throughout your house
(essential to good Feng Shui),
walk through your house. If
YOU can't flow freely through
the house (without tripping
on stuff), neither can energy.
Remove unneeded articles.
Simplify.

We Agree—Simplify!

Good Duct Shui suggests that you limit your toolbox to two items: duct tape and WD-40®. If it's not stuck and it's supposed to be, duct tape it. If it's stuck and it's not supposed to be, WD-40® it. Taking that into account, what other tools do you need? Simplify.

If your bathroom door is bigger than your bedroom door, you may have problems with your health, wealth, or marriage.

DUCT
SHUI
HOME

FENG SHUI RAY SEZ:

"Skip the expense of a marriage counselor and sink that same money into installing a garage door in your bedroom. This will also come in handy when it's time to move your bedroom furniture."

Discount Doors

If your bathroom door is bigger than your bedroom door, it probably means that you got mismatched doors from the discount building surplus warehouse. Which, yes, probably indicates that you are having problems with your wealth. This can be remedied by fixing more stuff with duct tape and not spending your money to bring in those overpriced "professionals."

The Cereal Solution

If you want your bathroom door to be smaller, duct tape cereal boxes around the perimeter. That way, the door is smaller, and if you get hungry in the middle of the night you won't have as far to walk to get some eats.

The Cereal Box Doorway Reducer

From Ray's
FENG⊙SHUI
Correspondence Manual

Windows that open outward will enhance the amount of positive energy that can enter a room. Windows that open inward can be harmful to careers and financial opportunities.

DUCT
SHUI
HOME

Shown on right: Jim insisted that we add his "Human Fly Terminator" idea. Duct tape flyswatters to your every extremity and flail about the room. Good idea, Jim.

Bug-Trapping Strips

Windows that open in any direction can maximize the number of bugs that come

into your home. To capture flying insects, hang strips of duct tape from the top of the window, sticky-side-out. The duct tape will capture bugs while still allowing air into the room.

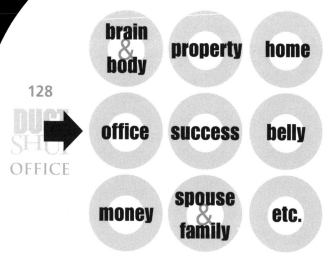

DUCT SHUI OFFICE

Achieving a sense of order and control in your workplace

You spend a lot of time at work. You can maximize your potential for success with a few simple applications of duct tape around your office.

From Ray's FENG SHUI Correspondence Manual

A fountain near the door of your office space will be a mood lifter and bring more salary your way. It will also diffuse the flow of bad chi (negative energy) into your office space.

DUCT SHUI OFFICE

FENG SHUI RAY SEZ:

"Hey, guys, while you work on your book, I'm gonna take a little nap. Wake me up when it's time to go bowling."

Keeping the Boss at Bay

To stop the flow of bad energy into your office (i.e., to keep the boss out of your cubicle), cover the entrance to your cubicle entirely in duct tape. Skip the fountain idea; that trickling sound will just make you have to go to the bathroom more (which may prove problematic with your door taped shut).

DUCT
SHUI
OFFICE

According to Feng Shui, the worst possible position for your office desk places your back to the door. This can be remedied by placing a mirror in front of you, positioned so that it reflects the door area.

Bad Office Desk Position

Look Out Behind You

Mirror, schmirror! Duct tape a video camera to your head and a monitor to your chest so you can always see who's behind you wherever you are.

If you are not this technologically inclined, you could just turn your desk around.

*The Duct Shui Cure for
Bad Office Desk Position*

134

DUCT
SHUI
OFFICE

If your office has a window directly behind you, it may create the feeling of vulnerability. Cure this situation by hanging a multifaceted crystal sphere about one third of the way down the window.

Bad Office Window Position

Create a Pleasing View

If your office has a window anyplace, you are luckier than most of us, so quit your complaining! If your office doesn't have a window, you can cure this situation by duct taping a large poster of a pleasant mountain scene on the wall and pretending you have an office in the Rockies.

Office "Poster Window"

DUCT SHUI OFFICE

From Ray's

FENG SHUI
Correspondence Manual

Mirrors placed to reflect each
other in an office can produce
feelings of expansion and
advancement.

DUCT
SHUI
OFFICE

FENG SHUI RAY SEZ:

"Did you ever go into one of them fancy
bathrooms that have mirrors on all the walls
and you look into the mirrors and there are like
about five hundred of you? That's pretty weird,
huh?"

Advance Yourself

To give yourself feelings of advancement, duct tape rearview mirrors to the sides of your head so you can see where you've been.

Or, you can make a little duct tape mark on the floor so you can turn around and see how far you've come.

Or, you can say to yourself "This is dumb!" and go bowling.

DUCT
SHUI
OFFICE

Mirrors Create the Illusion of a Larger You

Look Absolutely Massive

Here's how to create a feeling of expansion: Duct tape mirrors at 45-degree angles on either side of your body and you will look three times larger to anyone approaching you.

It also creates a feeling of expansion if you buy your pants one size too small.

DUCT
SHUI
OFFICE

140

DUCT
SHUI
OFFICE

If your office is too close to another building (especially a taller one), it creates feelings of oppression and victimization.

Ba-Gua mirror

To remedy this situation, put a Ba-Gua mirror on the outside wall or roof of your office building closest to the offending structure.

Another Page from Ray's Manual Showing a Ba-Gua Mirror (Again)

Block Negative Energy

Completely block negative energy by wrapping your entire office in duct tape (two or three layers may be necessary, depending on the size of neighboring buildings). Not only will the duct tape block the negative energy, your new "vinyl siding" means you won't have to paint your office for years.

Superiority on a Roll

To create feelings of superiority and authority, carry at least five rolls of duct tape strapped to your belt at all times. (Guys: Caution—wear a cup! Duct tape rolls swinging in the "frontal regions" can bring feelings of oppression and victimization.)

DUCT
SHUI
OFFICE

Anyone can possess a look of superiority, confidence, and pride when they have rolls of duct tape strapped to their sides.

Montage of Two Illustrations and Text

From Ray's

FENG⊙SHUI
Correspondence Manual

A metal wind chime in the front area of your office will summon people to help you.

DUCT
SHUI
OFFICE

AMAZING
FACT

111,111,111 x 111,111,111 =
12,345,678,987,654,321
What does this have to do with
Duct Shui? Absolutely nothing.
Nevertheless, it is an AMAZING FACT.

Enough with the Chimes!

If you put metal wind chimes in the front area of your office, you will indeed summon people—people who are angry about the constant tinkly-clinking coming from the front area of your office. An appropriate way to summon people to help you in the office is to ask politely for their help and then to reward them with a little roll of duct tape for their efforts.

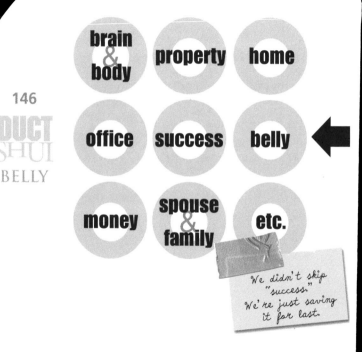

DUCT SHUI

BELLY

brain & body

property

home

office

success

belly

money

spouse & family

etc.

We didn't skip "success." We're just saving it for last.

DUCT SHUI BELLY

Duct Shui in the most important room of the house

One should never minimize the importance of the kitchen. No, you can't EAT duct tape, but it does come in quite handy around the kitchen. Go make yourself a sandwich and settle down in your favorite chair while we explain **Duct Shui for the Belly.**

From Ray's
FENG☯SHUI
Correspondence Manual

DUCT
SHUI
BELLY

A kitchen immediately visible
upon entering the front door of
your house can relate to a number
of health issues, including
digestion problems and binge
eating. The cure is to hang
a wind chime over the stove.

FENG SHUI RAY SEZ:

"Hey, Tim. You're out of potato chips."

DuCT SHUI COROLLARY

Point the Way to the Food

If your kitchen is not immediately visible when entering the front door of your house, your priorities are in the wrong place. You can "cure" this by putting big duct tape arrows on the walls pointing the way to the kitchen.

Point the Way to the Kitchen

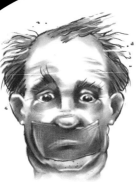

Duct Shui
Binge Eating Cure

Cure for Binge Eating

The cure for binge eating and digestive problems lies in duct tape placed firmly across your mouth. Or, if the whole family is dieting, wrap your refrigerator in four or five rolls of duct tape.

Flee Danger

The sight of Jim cooking (see below) is absolutely a forewarning of impending digestive problems. Do yourself a favor: Leave the house immediately and eat at your favorite restaurant.

Jim Serving His "Famous"
Clean-the-Fridge Burger

DUCT SHUI BELLY

Gas stoves put more positive chi into your food. Electric stoves cook with a hot electrical field, which produces low-quality food energy and exposes the cook and family to electrical fields. Microwave ovens are even worse. To remedy this bad energy, hang a multifaceted crystal sphere above the electric stove or microwave.

No Stove Necessary

Who needs a stove when you have duct
tape? Simply start a campfire (outdoors is
preferable to indoors) and dangle your
food over the fire with a strip of duct tape
until it is done (or drops into the fire when
the tape melts). If this doesn't work, do
what we do: Have a pizza delivered.

BELLY

Energize Your Food—Part One

Following the Feng Shui idea of putting energy into your food, we came up with this simple plan: Duct tape one end of a copper wire to the food you want to energize. Run the wire out your window and up the side of your house. Duct tape the other end to your chimney. Then, just sit back and wait for an electrical storm.

DUCT SHUI BELLY

ENERGY

TO CHIMNEY

COPPER WIRE

Food Being Naturally Energized

Energize Your Food—Part Two

Or, mix half a bottle of Tabasco® sauce and a mess of sliced-up jalapeño peppers into your food.

To avoid having your tongue melted and a hole burned in your stomach lining, wrap your food in little duct tape packets prior to swallowing it.

Person of Scandinavian Descent Eating Energized Food

DUCT
SHUI
BELLY

If your stove is too close to your refrigerator, you might experience health and wealth problems due to the conflict of hot and cold energy. Cure this problem by mirroring the side of the refrigerator to create the illusion of a larger stove area. Or, if there is a small counter between the stove and refrigerator, place small potted plants there to act as an energy buffer between the two opposing appliances.

More Counter Space

If your stove is too close to your refrigerator, the major problem as we see it is that you will not have enough counter space between the two appliances on which to prepare your meals. This could result in both frustrating hunger problems and a lot of spilled food ending up in the little crack between the stove and refrigerator. First, we suggest sealing up the crack with duct tape to prevent the inadvertent introduction of food and beverage onto your kitchen floor. Second, we suggest that you create more counter space by using duct tape and a cookie sheet or hunk of plywood to build a hinged counter that folds down over two of your stove burners. After all, who really uses four burners all the time? Caution: Duct tape over the control knobs to ensure that the burners under your new fold-down counter are kept in the "off" position.

By the way, hot and cold energy conflicts can be easily remedied by duct taping some fiberglass batting onto the side of the heat source for additional insulation.

Note: Sorry about the fine print. We didn't want to waste two pages on this stove stuff. But it does kind of look like an appliance warranty, doesn't it?

From Ray's
FENG SHUI
Correspondence Manual

Knives that are visible in the kitchen symbolize accidents. This is cured by keeping your knives in a drawer out of sight.

DUCT
SHUI
BELLY

DuCT
SHUI
COROLLARY

Symbolize This...

Duct tape that is visible throughout the house symbolizes resourcefulness, preparedness, and Duct Shui enlightenment.

Knife Control

Sharp knives can be kept as safe as butter knives by duct taping over their blades until you are ready to use them. *Refer to (A) below.*

To free up counter space, simply make a little knife pocket with duct tape and stick it under one of your upper cupboards. *Refer to (B) below.*

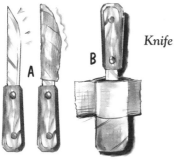

Knife Control

160

**DUCT
SHUI**
BELLY

Use all of the burners on your
stove. If you use only two or
three of your four burners, you
will have financial problems.
Since the burners represent the
wealth-generating potential of
your home, you need to rotate
the use of all burners to keep
money coming in regularly.

Burner Rotation Chart

If you choose to ascribe to the Feng Shui burner rotation theory, we suggest that you duct tape this handy little *burner rotation chart* next to your stove controls.

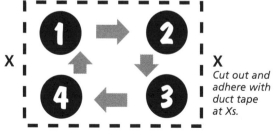

X

X
Cut out and adhere with duct tape at Xs.

What? No Recipes?

We were astounded that in all of the Feng Shui books we read for this project, we did not find one recipe. In fact, these Feng Shui guys only mention food in passing as a way that the body gets chi (energy)—duh.

We think it would be downright irresponsible of us if we didn't give you one recipe in this book, so here it is . . .

(For more of our favorite recipes, go to www.ducttapeguys.com.)

FENG SHUI RAY SEZ:

"What d'ya got to eat around here?"

Duct Shui turns ordinary canned baked beans into gourmet baked beans in minutes!

Duct Shui Baked Beans

Ingredients:

- 1 small onion (diced)
- 5 cloves garlic (sliced)
- ½ stick butter
- 1 big can baked beans
- 2 tablespoons brown sugar
- 1 tablespoon white vinegar
- ¼ can beer

Saute onion and garlic in butter until onions are translucent. Add other ingredients and stir over medium heat until the mixture bubbles. Serve on a duct tape–lined paper plate. Ummmm! Them's good eatin'!

Using Your Belly for Monetary Gain

DUCT
SHUI
BELLY

To keep money coming in regularly, we suggest that you wrap your bare belly with duct tape, sticky-side-out, and stand on a busy street corner asking people to stick paper money to you.

Warning: If you do not wrap all sides of your body, you'll be missing some of the passersby and thereby not achieve your maximum wealth-generating potential.

STICK ME WITH YOUR SPARE CASH

Note: This perfect transition from the "Belly" section to the "Money" section did not happen because of luck—it happened because of the diligent practice of Duct Shui in our lives. Honest!

Tape Your Torso and Wait for Riches

DUCT
SHUI
MONEY

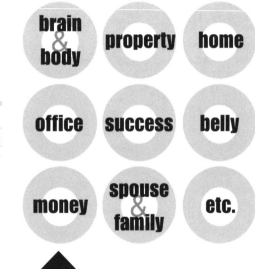

DUCT SHUI MONEY

How to attain, retain, and maximize your wealth through Duct Shui

Money may be the root of all evil, but that doesn't mean we don't need adequate quantities of the stuff to survive in today's world.

DUCT
SHUI
MONEY

To prevent your finances from becoming drained, keep your bathroom doors closed. Cover sink and tub drains, and keep the toilet seats down. Also put full-length mirrors outside of bathroom doors to reflect the energy away from the bathroom.

Don't Lose Loose Loot

If you're losing finances into the
toilet, you may not be lowering
your pants far enough before
you sit. To prevent the loss of
loose change, put a strip of
duct tape over each pocket
opening. Better still, keep
your money safely tucked
away under a duct tape
money belt.

Duct Tape Money Belt

Calculate the Savings

If you really want to prevent your finances from being drained, quit hiring expensive professionals to fix stuff—just do it yourself with duct tape. Plumber = $150 per hour. Roll of duct tape = about $4. You do the math *(see sample calculation on right)*.

Install a full-length mirror in your workshop so you can see yourself saving thousands with duct tape.

DUCT SHUI

MONEY

Duct Shui Saves $$$!
CALCULATE the SAVINGS

Here is an example of the savings you can experience by fixing a broken pipe yourself using duct tape:

Directory assistance to look up plumber's phone **75¢.**

Plumber's rate $150 per hour X 2 hours travel time plus 30 minutes under sink = **$375.00.**

Plumber material charge (new pipe and pipe compound) **$30.00** (reflects 600% markup from hardware store price)

Replace kitchen carpeting because of water damage due to prolonged wait time prior to repair **$850.00.**

Total cost of repair: **$1255.75**

Cost to repair with duct tape (1/2 roll required) **$2.50**

Time to repair, 10 minutes (no carpet damage).

Total Duct Shui Savings: $1253.25

Disposable Income

Speaking of toilets. . . . Before your child is potty trained, you can save big money on diapers by placing duct tape around the waistband and leg holes of the diaper. Those disposables that say "good for eight to ten pounds" now hold twenty to thirty pounds.

Or, make your own disposables: Just duct tape over multiple layers of paper toweling wrapped around baby's bottom.

DUCT SHUI
MONEY

Fishing for Financial Gain

Our experiences say that most finances are lost into the couch cushions. This can be avoided by duct taping your pockets shut. And, money can be retrieved by taping around a yardstick, sticky-side-out, and poking around the couch and chair cushion cracks.

Duct Tape Money Retriever

From Ray's
FENG⊙SHUI
Correspondence Manual

A fountain near the front door of your home will bring you more money and contact with influential people.

174

DUCT
SHUI
MONEY

AMAZING
FACT

If you have three quarters, four dimes, and four pennies, you have $1.19. You also have the largest amount of money in coins without being able to make change for a dollar. What does this have to do with Duct Shui? Again, nothing. Still, it is an AMAZING FACT.

A Fount of Admiration

Duct tape around the front door of your home will bring you the admiration of all those around you. Plus, you'll save money by not having to paint the door frame.

Wrap Up Big Savings

Want more money? Wrap your credit cards in four yards of duct tape. Not only will you have a convenient pocket-sized pack of duct tape, the duct tape will render your credit cards virtually useless. You will save thousands of dollars in no time!

MONEY

From Ray's
FENG SHUI
Correspondence Manual

Improve your luck, bring wealth and prosperity by reciting this mantra: Gate gate, Para gate, Para sum gate, Bodhi swaha. (Pronunciation: GAH-tay GAH-tay, PAIR-uh GAH-tay, PAIR-uh SUM GAH-tay, BOH-dee SWA-ha.)

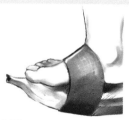

Figure 176: Unrelated Illustration Number One

DuCT SHUI COROLLARY

Luck on a Roll

Luck? With duct tape, you don't need luck. Just a little ingenuity and you will be well on your way to wealth and prosperity.

If you are like us, and we know we are, the mere utterance of the words *Duct Tape* (pronunciation: DAHk-tAPE) will make you feel prosperous.

Note: Careful readers will recognize the mantra on the left as the same mantra Feng Shui uses to help you perform better in daily life. Pretty versatile mantra, huh? Either that, or they just aren't that creative.

If your front entry leads to a playroom or game room, you may experience rapid financial fluctuations. Cure this by hanging a crystal sphere three feet inside the front door.

178

DUCT SHUI

MONEY

*A Duct-Tape-Covered Birdcage
May Work in Lieu of a Crystal*

No Strangers to Financial ~~Flatulence~~ Fluctuation

If your front entry leads to a playroom or game room, you probably live with one of The Duct Tape Guys. The cure for this is to build your own playroom or game room near your own front door—since our rapid financial fluctuations are not conducive to having a lot of people living with us.

179

DUCT
SHUI
MONEY

Control Your Impulse to Wager

DUCT
SHUI
MONEY

Game rooms associated with rapid financial fluctuations says one thing: gambling addiction. Our cure is to wrap your wallet with three yards of duct tape to curb your gambling impulse.

Speaking of gambling . . . Reno, Nevada, is west of Los Angeles, California.

Bonus Money-Saving Hint

If you have been a victim of a vending machine that takes your money and gives you nothing in return, here's your chance to get even and save money at the same time. Simply attach duct tape to your dollar

bill. Let it feed into the bill reader, then quickly pull it back out. Get the "hook up" for free pop, free food, and free change!

DUCT
SHUI
MONEY

INSERT BILL HERE

Editor's note: Jim and Tim (still performing community service) asked me to mention that this hint might not be advisable.

182

DUCT
SHUI
MONEY

A fish tank containing eight orange goldfish and one black goldfish placed in the hsun (southwest) position of your living room will bring wealth.

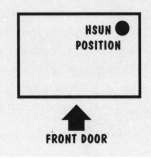

Page from Ray's Manual Showing Hsun Position

DUCT SHUI
COROLLARY

Boiled Fish?

A fish tank placed in direct sunlight often results in boiled fish. Duct tape over the top of your fish tank to prevent the odor of dead fish from filling your room when you inevitably sun-boil or overfeed them.

DUCT SHUI
MONEY

The fish taco, while it sounds disgusting, is very popular in some parts of the country.

Kill-Proof Fish

Skip the fish and make little duct tape fish-shaped things that you can stick on the wall of your living room. This will affect your financial situation positively in that you won't be shelling out the big bucks for aquarium supplies and fish food.

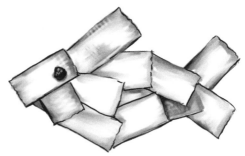

Duct Tape Fish

FINANCIAL PLANNING WORKSHEET

Make a list of what you will do with all the money
you'll save by incorporating our Duct Shui ideas.

**DUCT
SHUI
MONEY**

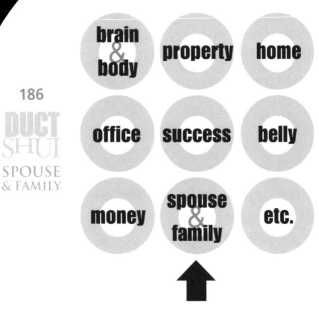

DUCT SHUI

SPOUSE & FAMILY

brain & body

property

home

office

success

belly

money

spouse & family

etc.

DUCT SHUI SPOUSE & FAMILY

Achieving marital bliss and family harmony through Duct Shui

Can duct tape positively influence your love life? How about your relationship with your kids or the in-laws? After studying these pages, we think you will say, "YES!"

From Ray's
FENG☯SHUI
Correspondence Manual

To liven up your love life,
place new plants (nine maximum)
in your bedroom. Plants with
pink flowers are more powerful.

DUCT
SHUI
SPOUSE
& FAMILY

AMAZING
FACT

Thirty-five percent of the people who
use personal ads for dating are
already married.

Duct Tape Proposal

The Duct Tape Guys only write G-rated books and calendars, so you can use your own imagination as to what to do with duct tape to liven up your love life. However, we have found that duct tape is a great way to pick up women. In fact, it was how Jim got his wife to accept his proposal of marriage. He simply duct taped himself to her leg until she said yes.

From Ray's
FENG☯SHUI
Correspondence Manual

The color of your bedsheets matters! Use pink sheets for love and romance, red for hot passion (change the color if you aren't getting enough sleep), green for money and good health, and yellow for healing.

FENG SHUI RAY SEZ:

"I use red plaid flannel sheets on my bed. They got all the colors in 'em except pink. Maybe that's why I ain't gettin' any romance."

Keeping the Bed Tidy

Duct tape is great if you live with a restless sleeper. Just duct tape the corners of the sheets under the mattress and they'll never pop out of place. If your spouse is extremely restless, you can duct tape him/her into place.

SPOUSE
& FAMILY

Note: Although duct tape does come in a complete array of colors, the color of duct tape doesn't matter (since you can't really see the colors in the dark anyway).

192

DUCT SHUI

SPOUSE
& FAMILY

Chinese energy theory suggests that as a woman conceives a child, the energy representing the new baby first forms underneath the bed. When the time is right, the fetal energy moves up into the woman's body. Therefore, it is unwise to clean under the bed while trying to conceive a child.

Prevent Conception

If this is true, then it makes sense to keep the floor under your bed clean when you are trying *not* to conceive a child. And what better way to do that than with duct tape? Wrap your small dog (borrow your neighbor's if you don't have one) in duct tape, sticky-side-out. Roll his toy under the bed and tell him to fetch. When he comes out from under the bed, all the dust bunnies will be stuck to the duct tape. Rewrap and repeat until no dust is visible.

SPOUSE
& FAMILY

Duct Cleaning

This same taped-dog hint can be used for cleaning out your furnace ductwork (saving you even more money—which causes us to think that you might want to remove this page and tape it into the "Money" section).

Warning: Make sure you turn off the furnace first. (Boy, that smell didn't go away for weeks.)

Back to Conception

Duct Shui theory suggests that when trying *not* to conceive a child, duct tape makes an excellent chastity belt. Nothing says "keep out" like a few well-placed strips of duct tape.

KEEP OUT

Duct Tape Chastity Belt

DUCT
SHUI

SPOUSE
& FAMILY

From Ray's
FENG SHUI
Correspondence Manual

A ceiling beam over your bed can result in marriage and health ailments. The best cure is to hang Feng Shui bamboo flutes at 45-degree angles at both ends of the beam.

DUCT
SHUI
SPOUSE
& FAMILY

AMAZING
FACT

On average, 100 people choke to death on ballpoint pens every year. Again, this has nothing to do with Feng Shui or Duct Shui. We just happened to see Ray sucking on a pen and thought we ought to warn you.

Bedroom Tape Storage

We have found that a ceiling beam over the bed is a great place to hang extra rolls of duct tape. That way, if you get a call in the middle of the night from someone who needs you to fix something, your tape is right there. And because you'll be able to find it in the dark, you won't need to turn on a light and awaken your spouse—which could result in marital disharmony.

SPOUSE
& FAMILY

You can uplift the chi of a lazy
person who spends too much time
in bed by placing a wind chime
in the center of the bedroom.

DUCT
SHUI
SPOUSE
& FAMILY

*Note: The first principle of Duct Shui is as follows:
"The lazier the person, the more they need Duct Shui."
Let the lazy person lie, provided he has performed all
of the Duct Shui activities that we have suggested in
this book.*

Awaken, O Sleeper!

If a person is spending too much time in bed, he is probably just too darned comfortable. Duct tape pots and pans from the ceiling and blow them against each other with an industrial-strength fan. When the duct tape eventually lets go, the pans will come crashing down on the sleeper, thereby motivating his exit from the bedchamber.

SPOUSE
& FAMILY

From Ray's
FENG☯SHUI
Correspondence Manual

If trees are healthy and lush around your house, it bodes well for your family. If the trees suddenly die, beware of an onslaught of bad luck.

DUCT SHUI

SPOUSE & FAMILY

AMAZING FACT

Speaking of bad luck . . . If you were unlucky enough to be born a major league baseball, your average lifespan is only seven pitches.

Flee Town!

If all of the trees around your house suddenly die, duct tape a gas mask to the face of every member of your family and flee town. Something bad, like a herbicide, is probably in the air.

Duct Shui Protection Suggestion

DUCT
SHUI
SPOUSE
& FAMILY

Resurrect Dead Trees

Dead trees can be made to look alive and vital with the application of green duct tape perma-leaves. Or, for that constant "colors of fall" look, use red, orange, and yellow duct tape.

Duct Tape Perma-Leaves

FAMILY CONVERSION CHECKLIST

A happy family is one that shares common beliefs.
Make a list of all your immediate and extended family
members in the space below. Check the names off as
you convert them into Duct Shui practitioners. (It helps
if you purchase a copy of this book for each of them.)

DUCT
SHUI
SPOUSE
& FAMILY

_____

_____

_____

_____

_____

_____

_____

_____

_____

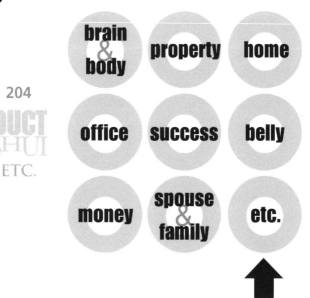

DUCT
SHUI
ETC.

Other stuff we thought of and couldn't fit in anywhere else

Etc.

DUCT
SHUI
ETC.

From Ray's
FENG☯SHUI
Correspondence Manual

Squeaky door hinges will attract real or imagined ghosts. Feng Shui experts suggest a liberal coating of WD-40® to silence the hinge.

DUCT SHUI ETC.

WD-40® was created by the Rocket Chemical Company in San Diego, CA, in 1953—the same year that Duct Shui Master Tim was born! WD-40® got its name from the fact that it was the 40th formulation of the Water Displacement fluid that worked.

Yin and Yang of Your Toolbox

We had no idea that they had WD-40® in ancient China! Well, we'll have to agree with the Feng Shui principle here. We've always contended that WD-40® and duct tape are the Yin and Yang of your toolbox. So, go ahead . . . spray those squeaky hinges with WD-40®. (And pick up your copy of our *WD-40 Book* at ducttapeguys.com.)

Duct Tape —— WD-40®

The Ridding of Ghosts

**DUCT
SHUI
ETC.**

To get rid of the ghosts that squeaking hinges may have attracted, simply bind yourself in duct tape, sticky-side-out, and flail around the house until all of the ghosts are stuck to the duct tape—then shed your "duct tape skin" in the bathroom, where the ghosts will be sucked into your drains and flushed into the storm sewer.

Note: If it is an imagined ghost that you're trying to rid the house of, just imagine yourself doing what we have just described.

Actual Photo of a Ghost Captured on Duct Tape

Never place a mirror opposite an open bedroom door, since it will reflect the incoming energy back out of the room.

210

DUCT
SHUI
ETC.

FENG SHUI RAY SEZ:

"Utilizing my powers of logic, I came to the conclusion that mirrors, hung backwards on walls, would suck energy into rooms. Now my house is filled with so much energy that I had to leave."

Speaking of Scary Stuff . . .

Never place a mirror opposite any open door. When you come home late at night, you will repeatedly startle yourself as you enter the room and see someone right in front of you! If such a mirror is not removable, duct tape over it to avoid this heart-stopping experience.

Unrelated Illustration Number Two

From Ray's
FENG SHUI
Correspondence Manual

Crystal balls hung from the rearview mirror of your car empower your car for safety and give you a feeling of calmness.

DUCT
SHUI
ETC.

AMAZING
FACT

Pound for pound, hamburgers cost more than new cars.

No More Fuzzy Dice

Duct tape rolls hung from the ceiling of your car tend to swing around, hitting you in the head. This is not necessarily safe, but it does produce feelings of euphoria.

Note: A crystal ball hanging from your rearview mirror will probably cause people to think you are "one of them New Age kooks." If you are insistent on hanging a ball in your car, make it a disco ball; that way, they'll just think you're spinning your wheels in the '70s.

From Ray's **FENG SHUI** Correspondence Manual

A flute can be used to drive away negative individuals.

DUCT SHUI ETC.

DUCT SHUI COROLLARY

Music played by Tim drives everyone away. *(Not a hint, just a fact.)*

We're sure that we didn't think of everything to throw into the "ETC." section. If you think of something, feel free to write it in the space below:

_____

_____

_____

_____

_____

_____

_____

_____

_____

_____

_____

215

DUCT
SHUI
ETC.

DUCT SHUI
SUCCESS

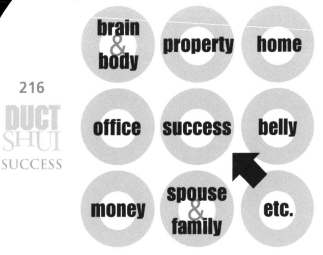

DUCT SHUI SUCCESS

How all of this stuff equals SUCCESS for YOU!

It's late in the book and we're running out of words. So . . . no further comment.

You *ARE* Successful!

If all the Duct Shui hints that you have read about in this book are followed, then you'll have achieved a degree of success.* In fact, even if you follow only one of them you may experience success.*/**

As Duct Shui tradition (albeit new) suggests, the more people you tell about Duct Shui and the more Duct Shui books that you purchase for your friends and relatives, the more popular*** and successful* you will become.**

**DUCT
SHUI
SUCCESS**

* Success as measured by Duct Tape Guy standards.
** Actual results may vary.
*** Your popularity with us, The Duct Tape Guys.
§ ‡ ∞ Other symbols not used here.

Friendly Measure of Success

If you measure success by the number of friends you have, Duct Shui lets you accumulate friends like nobody's business. No, we don't mean accumulating friends by duct taping yourself sticky-side-out and bumping into people (although Tim, in his high school years, actually resorted to this on a couple of occasions). We're talking about the accumulation of friends by belonging to a brotherhood (or sisterhood, for you gals) of duct tape enthusiasts. This is a wholesome group that even your mother would be proud to belong to.

Label Your Storage Shed Success

If you measure success by the amount of stuff you own, duct tape is essential. Following the old Duct Shui adage, "It ain't broke, it just lacks duct tape," you can accumulate LOTS of stuff because:

1) You have the one tool and the skills necessary to fix items that other people would have discarded.
2) You will have saved money by repairing items instead of replacing them, thus allowing you to . . .
3) Purchase more stuff that you will eventually repair with duct tape—starting the cycle all over again.

Family Ties = Success

If you measure success by your marital and family happiness, we don't know of anything that can make a family stick together better than the common bond of duct tape.

(At this juncture, you may wish to reread the "Spouse & Family" section as a refresher. In fact, gather the whole family together and read it aloud.)

**DUCT
SHUI
SUCCESS**

Success = No Enemies

If you measure your degree of success by your lack of enemies, remember, you can always make friends by the simple act of sharing your duct tape.

Speaking of enemies, if there are die-hard Feng Shui disciples out there who have been offended by our comparisons and interpretations . . . well, sorry. If your Feng works for you as well as our Duct works for us, you have found your own degree of success and we are happy for you.

> *Did that sound sincere, Jim?*
> Huh? I wasn't listening.
> *Never mind.*

Become a Duct Shui Master

To achieve the certification of Duct Shui Master, follow these simple steps:

1) Read this book.
2) Use duct tape at least once per day.
3) Tell others about Duct Shui.
4) Download your official Duct Shui Master certificate from our web site: www.ducttapeguys.com/ductshui

DUCT TAPE PRO.

DUCT SHUI MASTER

This diploma certifies that

Your Name Here

has satisfactorily completed all requirements necessary to have attained the highly respected certification of Duct Shui™ Master and is hereby officially licensed to teach the philosophy of Duct Shui.

Not valid without this official seal.

Dualy signed and certified by Duct Shui Masters, Jim and Tim

VISIT

www.ducttapeguys.com

the DUCT TAPE GUYS

The duct tape fun never stops at The Duct Tape Guys' web site. Stop by for more Duct Tape Guy wit and wisdom.* You can purchase Duct Tape Pro™ apparel, join our free e-newsletter, enter contests, and share *your* duct tape stories. ***Visit us today!***

*Wisdom is subject to change without notice.